WORDS FROM WITHIN

KENYA WILLIAMS

WORDS FROM WITHIN

ACCEPTANCE

Lord,
I accept Your will through the good, bad,
The ugly, even to the worst.
I thank You for allowing me
to experience these things.
Knowing what I know now,
Life is only a test.
For each test, I grow stronger
and wiser by the day.
Thanks to family, friends, and loved ones.
From the highest to the lowest part of life.
I will always accept God as my Lord and Saver.

TABLE OF CONTENTS

. . . .

AS A CHILD

Lonely as a child,
I needed my mother's touch and love.
Growing up without my family,
I struggled a lot with abandonment issues.
I felt like no one cared enough for me.
I was brought to a city with only a few
relatives.
Living in a fast-paced environment,
I had to adapt for survival.
Forced to stand my ground.

As a child, I felt so alone.
I didn't have anyone to take up for me.
I became a fighter—
Someone who wouldn't give up!
I fought my way out of loneliness,
depression, and neglect.

I dealt with a lot of anger and disappointment,
I had resentment toward my parents.
I didn't understand as a child,
Why did I have to move away?
Growing up was so difficult,
Adapting to a new environment
and being surrounded by strangers.
I felt like I was an estranged child,
Far away from home, deserted
and not wanted.

As a child in disbelief,
Hoping my parents would be together,
Praying for my past to be altered,
Having a belief that it was all a dream.
Maybe one day, I'll wake up from the
nightmare.

As a child,
Wanting to hug my mom,
Be with my mom,

Even cried for my mom.
Feeling out of place, I created a place.
A place where I would sketch my
way through misery,
Drawing favorite cartoon characters
and superheroes.
I found a way to cope with the
absence of affection.
In my imaginary world, I was the hero.
I didn't need anyone anymore.

As a child, I was a loner.
I crossed paths with many friends,
And I became one with myself.
I began to lead and care for others.
Along the way, I became a brother to others.
Being embraced by neighbors
and their families.
They showed me love and compassion,
Allowing me to be a part of their family.
The temporary loss of my family

Taught me to be independent and
to depend on myself.
On many occasions, I fought
and stood up to bullies in school.

As a child,
Being by myself was normal.
I had no siblings around to laugh,
argue, and play fight with.
Most of my time was spent hanging
around with the kids from the block.
They were my brothers and cousins,
My family away from my family.
I learned survival tactics.
The first lesson was on boxing
and how to defend myself.

As a child, I learned,
In life, you get knocked down and you get
back up.
God puts us in situations
To strengthen us in character and faith.

As a child,
I've grown into a strong and wiser person.

GOD

. . . .

Dear Father,
I know You are looking down on me.
People have been talking down on me.
Send me a blessing from above,
So I can live like the doves and be free.
That breeze that would guide me
To the mountains where the clouds are bright
So when night falls, I will eternally shine.
In vain, I will live without shame.
I'm Your child!
I'm not afraid to say it,
And I won't hide it.
A father who can do wonders,
He will lead you right;
Never will He guide you wrong.
When you are feeling alone,
God is there all the time.

Always by your side at any given time
He is with you through the rain,
sleet, and snow.
He's always there!
His presence is near.
Can't see with your eyes,
But you can visualize it with your heart.
God is with you from beginning until the end.
Start to finish, He is with you.
God loves us all the time
His spirit shines in us all.

REPENT

. . . .

Must we repent?
Of course!
Let's wash all our sins away.
So we can live with faith
That one day
God will return.
When that day comes,
We all must pray,
"Now I lay me down to sleep.
I pray the Lord my soul to keep.
If I should die before I wake,
I pray the Lord my soul to take."

God,
I know you are looking down on me
I know when the ground is touched by You,
The flowers will bloom,

The sun will shine,
The leaves will flow,
The wind will blow.
Trees will grow,
Birds will sing,
Children will swing.

Babies play,
Balloons are in the air,
Love is everywhere.

Cheers and praises!
The man upstairs has come
And all power is in His hands.
God, our Heavenly Father,
In Jesus' name I pray,

Amen.

ON MY OWN

In this world all alone,
This road I must cross.
 Friends are so overrated.
I'm on my own.

So I can stand firm,
Surrounded by these concrete walls.
Trapped by betrayal, jealousy and hatred.
I'm on my own.

Like a dream that won't go away,
How far must I go?
 When will I reach that pot of gold?
Suffering from the flames of life.
The tears I cry when this brain of mine will fry.
Will the pain ever stop?

TRYING TO LIVE

. . . .

Trying to live is the most important
thing in the world to me.
Trying to live through all the pain and
suffering…
Trying to live one day at a time.
Things for me began to go wrong.
I don't understand why things won't go right.
I'm trying to live the best I know how.
Trying to live is the most important thing
in the world to me.

ILLNESS

. . . .

*This poem goes out to thousands of people with the
illness called Sickle Cell Anemia.*

To a special person who means the
world to me.
I don't come around as much as I used to.
She's family, more than that, she's a friend.
I've been thinking of her lately.
So for her, I wrote this poem.
I know it's hard so don't cry.
Be strong, God watches all.
Never give up on your hopes and dreams,
Pray and God will carry you through.
Don't lose faith, God will make a way
for this illness.
Keep that heart of yours and depart
from this illness of yours.

Below you is the ground, don't frown now,
Look up and smile,
Give thanks to the man above.
You've made it this far, keep the
faith God is always near
My dear, don't feel depressed.
Your blessings are still here.

MAMA

. . . .

I thank you for all you have done.
Without you, I would probably be alone.
When I'm broke, you're always here to
give me a loan.
I'll never be alone, as long as I have you.

Just when things are bad,
you know the words that make me glad.
I can never be sad with a Mama like you.

You show love and protection;
Your love is like no other.
I'm thankful for all you've done.
No one could ever replace you.

I love you, Mama.
You're always on my mind,

I speak to you from the heart.
I feel sad when we are apart.
Never feel bad…Be glad
Your son has grown into a man.

Mama,
Don't ever forget that I love you for life.
So smile, this is for you!
Nobody else but you.
I love you when the sun rises.
I love you when the moon falls.
I love you, Mama!

FATHER

. . . .

I love when he's around!
Life is much happier when he is here.
I feel strong, secure, and fearless
within his presence.
I enjoy the time we spend together,
A chance to say what's on my mind.
Even though his time is worth more
than a dime.
He's that number one guy.
How can I ever repay him?
I am a better man myself…
He made me into the man I am today.
I love when he's around.
He changed my sadness to happiness.

I CRY

. . . .

Lord, I cry Your name!
It's a shame, I know.
I cry Your name in vain.

My problems have gotten worse.
I need something to enlighten my soul.
I'm lost; there's no one I can trust, but You.
I cry because things are not the same.
Life is still a game.

I cry for guidance—
A guidance to lead me to righteousness.
I live for the best,
But sometimes I feel the worst
All I ask is for a happy home,
If not, send me on my way.
At least a faraway place where I can be happy.

Lord, will the problems ever end?
I cried for a road of joy.
When I reach that road of peace and
Then the mess will decrease.

Lord, I cry Your name!
From the beginning to the end, I cry.
Can you feel Kenya's cry?

MY AUNT

. . . .

The sweetest person
I love her so
I give thanks to her everyday

My aunt
I thank you
For caring and praying for me
When I was down and troubled

My aunt
Was unconditionally there
When I was in need of understanding
Her heart did wonders to my life
Even when no one else was around

My aunt
Was always there
I'm impressed!
She was one of the best

My aunt
Is the sweetest person I know
I love her so

WONDER

. . . .

At night, I sit and wonder,
What am I going to be in life?
What does the Lord have in store for me?
I guess in reality, life is what you make it.
But sometimes I feel like this dream is
not too far,
Because it's in my heart and people
love to talk.

In this world,
There are no friends. Sometimes family
is all I have,
Even though family treats you like the enemy.

In this world,
The only one I can trust is God.
Father, mother, sister, or brother…

None of them can help me reach this
goal of mine.
Nobody but me and only me can
reach the top.
I know that jealousy will not stop.
The attitude I have will carry me through
this dream I have.

I write to express and not to impress.
I do what's best for me and not for
so-called friends.
When I'm broken down and alone,
God is the only one I can call.

I've learned in this world,
There are a lot of people who love me,
And a lot of people who hate me.
But I treat them all with respect.

I don't ask for anything,
I just want peace of mind.

I look to the sun because one day I know
I'm going to shine.

I feel like crying and I use the only gift
I have to get me through.

Lord, please
I ask in Your name
Give me a chance to make it in this world
As life spins around.
I need Your help to get rid of the negativity,
hurt, and the pain.
I pray for better days.
I show love not just to You but to those
who hate me too.

This writing is the reason my faith is so strong,
It's hard, tough, and rough
But my heart is solid.
I know it won't break me,
It will only make me stronger.

I wonder why I must go through life
facing these temptations,
That are here everyday.
I guess that's why it's called trials and
tribulations.

I get so frustrated thinking of the
times people used and abused me.
But I see it as just the beginning.

Lord, I wonder
After the rain fall
Will I be able to stand?

EVERYDAY I THANK GOD

. . . .

Every day, I thank God,
Because without Him life would be a struggle.
Life would be harder without the help of God.

Every day, I thank God.
Look at all the things He has given me!
A caring family, a job, a home, and finances.
I know He wouldn't have brought me this far if
He didn't care

Every day, I think God,
Because without Him life would be a struggle.

ESCAPE

It's hard to escape the sins of life.
No matter how hard I try,
The snake of the enemy
Wants to wrap itself around me,
Squeezing and pulling me back
To this dark place I don't want to be.
Every time I break free,
It slithers its way back.
I pray for an escape
Because each turn feels like a maze.
A crowd of snakes coming in all directions
I have no choice but to fight.
Swallowed and digested by this
conniving spirit,
Faith is my weapon of choice
As I hatched my way through the
belly of the beast.

Life's a survival on a quest for redemption,
Sawing my way through the toughest skin
Only to find peace and prosperity.
Lord!
I shall fear no evil.
Covered in Your blood,
I escaped the enemy's den.

HE'LL MAKE
A WAY

. . . .

When things seem to get hard,
He'll make a way.

Sometimes I know people can do wrong.
Pray, and he'll make a way.

If you do what's right,
He'll make a way.

When the going gets tough,
He'll make a way for you.

Lord!

We'll make all things possible,
If you believe.

He'll never mistreat you,
He'll make a way for us all.

He'll make a way through the toughest times.
He'll bring light to the deepest night.

I can never lose with God on my side,
He's my knight in shining armor.

So when life gets hard,
He'll make a way!

DON'T CRY

. . . .

Don't cry, dry your eyes.
Wipe your tears away.
Don't feel sad,
Your friend is with you all the time.
Look to the stars because
Your friend has touched the sky.
Another soul is taken,
Another heart is broken.
Have faith and your heart will heal.

Stay strong.
Don't cry, dry your eyes.
Wipe the tears away.
Your friend is in a faraway place.

NO MORE
LONELY TEARS

. . . .

I know how it feels to lose someone special,
A person close to you
Another soul has gone
And it's time to move on.

Be strong.
Your sister is now in a better place,
A place where she is now at ease.
I know it's hard to say goodbye.
Ask the Lord how,
He will show you the way.

Pray and everything will be alright.
It's okay to cry, but do it because
you are happy.

I know it's sad when someone leave so early.
Remember she's here in the spirit,
In the heart and in the mind.
Wash those tears away.

ANGEL

. . . .

This angel of mine
Will come at any time
She will always shine
I dream of this angel all the time
She is in my mind
She is a beauty of love, a daughter of God
She is Jesus' little princess
This angel is special
She is loving, caring, and outgoing
I carry her in my mind, heart, body, and soul
She is never forgotten
She is my lady of joy, my lady of love,
A lady of happiness and a lady of inspiration
This angel inspires me
She loved me, believed in me, took care of me,
Helped raise, comfort and nurse me
It hurts knowing that she isn't here

Even though she's gone,
Her spirit remains deep inside
I know she will forever shine in my life
Until the day I die
She would always be my shining star,
The light in my heart, an angel who
is not too far
An angel that's in the sky
my aunt, this angel of mine
May God bless her

GRANDMA

. . . .

The heart to everyone's family.
The best cook,
Teacher, Caretaker,
Disciplinarian.
The mother of all moms.
There is nothing I wouldn't do to get one hug.
I miss your love, your tenderness and kisses.
Reminiscing of the good times,
Keeping us inline with your switch,
With that famous line "Get your blank
out of here!"
Funny to us but loving in a cheerful way.

Grandma, a woman of wisdom and faith.
She prayed day in and day out
for the safety of her children,
The rock to every household,

The strength to every family,
The key to the foundation.

Grandma,
The lifeline to each family tree,
Each vessel to life
She's the definition of family values,
The backbone to the family legacy.
Thanks for the life you lived,
The prayers you made,
The love you gave,
The values instilled in us.

Grandma

WORDS FROM WITHIN

. . . .

I can't take no more!
Time is running out.
Life is too short to worry
About the things that are wrong.
Why does a person like me
Go through so much as a child?
I can't understand
Why I was treated so badly.
It's sad.
All I want is a chance to live,
No wrong intentions.
Family can put you through so much pain.
How could a family do such a thing?
I know that words can be powerful.
Express how you feel and let it go.

Speak now or forever hold your peace.
Take these words I say seriously,
Our lives have already been written

LIFE

. . . .

Life can throw a curveball
If you're not careful.
We must continue with the race
And jump over the hurdles in life.

The finish line of fulfilment is yards away.
Push and push until you can't push any more.
Breath after breath,
Stroke after stroke.
Stay focused on life's destiny.

People will throw stones and talk about you.
Continue on the pursuit towards happiness.
When God's for you, who can be against you?
Go full speed ahead, the finish
line is just a few steps away.

Lord!!!
My life is going in circles.
Lap after lap.
I'm on that home stretch,
Sweating and trying to catch my breath,
Wobbling and trying to keep my balance.

As the wind whispers,
Stay on the track.
Life's the victory lane
Through the finish line victory
is finally all mine!

PROSPER

. . . .

Through all the pain and suffering,
I have prospered!
I have come a long way—
From being alone to being strong.

I have prospered!
When I was cold and all alone,
God would hold and carry me.
On the street,
I learned to stand on my own.

I have prospered!
Life is a growing experience.
Everyone can prosper from it.
I was taught two wrongs don't make it right.
If you're not careful it can lead to a fight.

I have prospered!
With God, our job is to love each other.
You and I both can prosper from that.
It took tears from my peers
For me to prosper from all my fears.
When I was blind, God planted a vision,
A reality that would come at night
Through all the pain and suffering.

I have prospered!
Prosper is something I've grown to do!

I THANK YOU

For the many blessings
The gift of foresight
Living this life as written
I'm a witness to Your grace
I've been left out to dry
Clotheslined by triumph
Knocked down and blown over by sin
Only to be clothespinned to life

I thank You
For the challenges and perseverance
I'm developing into a warrior of faith
As a disciple, I march for greatness
In this battle of living
Hand to hand combat against destruction
Making it through defeat
Gaining the strength to conquer

This spiritual war

I thank You
For shielding me from this army
That's out to destroy me
Cover and protect me
Lord, I thank You
For placing Your hands on me
 Life is a constant battle

FORGIVENESS

I pray that You will forgive me
For all the wrongs I've done
My past wasn't the best
I've said and done things
I shouldn't have
I prayed for a change
 Given a second chance
Has been a continuous fight
I'm fighting for my peace, soul, mind and spirit
Breaking the chains to sanity
Holding on to this rope for dear life
Trying not to lose my grip
I struggle to climb reaching for that sense of
forgiveness
Pull by pull the stronger I get
Trouble begins to crumble down
by the wayside

The more I climb, the more my feet slip, the more problems fall
Lord! Have mercy on me
I fall short of weakness and breath
Pushing to overcome this mountain
Slowly I see the sun clearer
Life gets brighter by the day
My peace is greater, soul, mind and spirit
Finally I've made it
Through the clouds the mountain view
Looking back over the years
I can say God brought me far
He's glorious
These are my steps to
Forgiveness

WALK AND BREATHE

. . . .

I give thanks to the Lord up above
For the many blessings He gave to me.
I love all my family and friends.
May God continue to guide us on
the right path.

Walk and breathe
Life is the only way.
Be happy with yourself.

MY TESTAMENT

. . . .

Lord, over the years,
I've come thus far.
Forgive me if I'm wrong,
I just wanna be whole.
I pray in Your name,
Because a lot has changed
People throwing dirt on my name, but
I'm not the one to blame.
When the fire is lit and the ashes are burned,
I pray for guidance.
You'll reshore my soul
And place me on a righteous path.

Amen!

THE THINGS I DO

. . . .

You can't even imagine the things I do.
The things I do are hard.
Growing up as a child,
I sometimes struggled to make a dime.
Trouble came daily with frustration.
I've found salvation in writing,
It satisfies my spirit.

My life has landed on this destination.
The things I do cause me to mature
And with that maturity comes wisdom.
After the wisdom, then knowledge cones.
Having the free will to think and do for myself.
I pray to God for good health and life!

I SEE

. . . .

I See
My third eye is open
The plan that's for me
Lord, it is all so clear
My purpose is before me

I See
The benefits of the future
Investing in my craft
Life's longevity

ABOUT THE
AUTHOR

. . . .

Kenya Williams is an author who loves music, poetry, and films. As a little child, Kenya began to write stories and poems. Infatuated by music lyrics and creative writing, Kenya was inspired to become a lyricist and writer. The best source of expression for Kenya is spoken word, a craft he has developed through childhood, hoping to inspire people.

**Follow Kenya on Instagram
@kenyawilliams13**

THANK YOU

. . . .

Thank you for joining me on this poetic journey. I pray something I shared will inspire you to open your heart and share your own message with the world.

If you enjoyed this book, please take a few moments to write a review on Amazon.

Kenya Williams

www.ingramcontent.com/pod-product-compliance
Lightning Source LLC
Chambersburg PA
CBHW060711030426
42337CB00017B/2836